To Grandma
with love,
Merry Christmas
1971

Sue

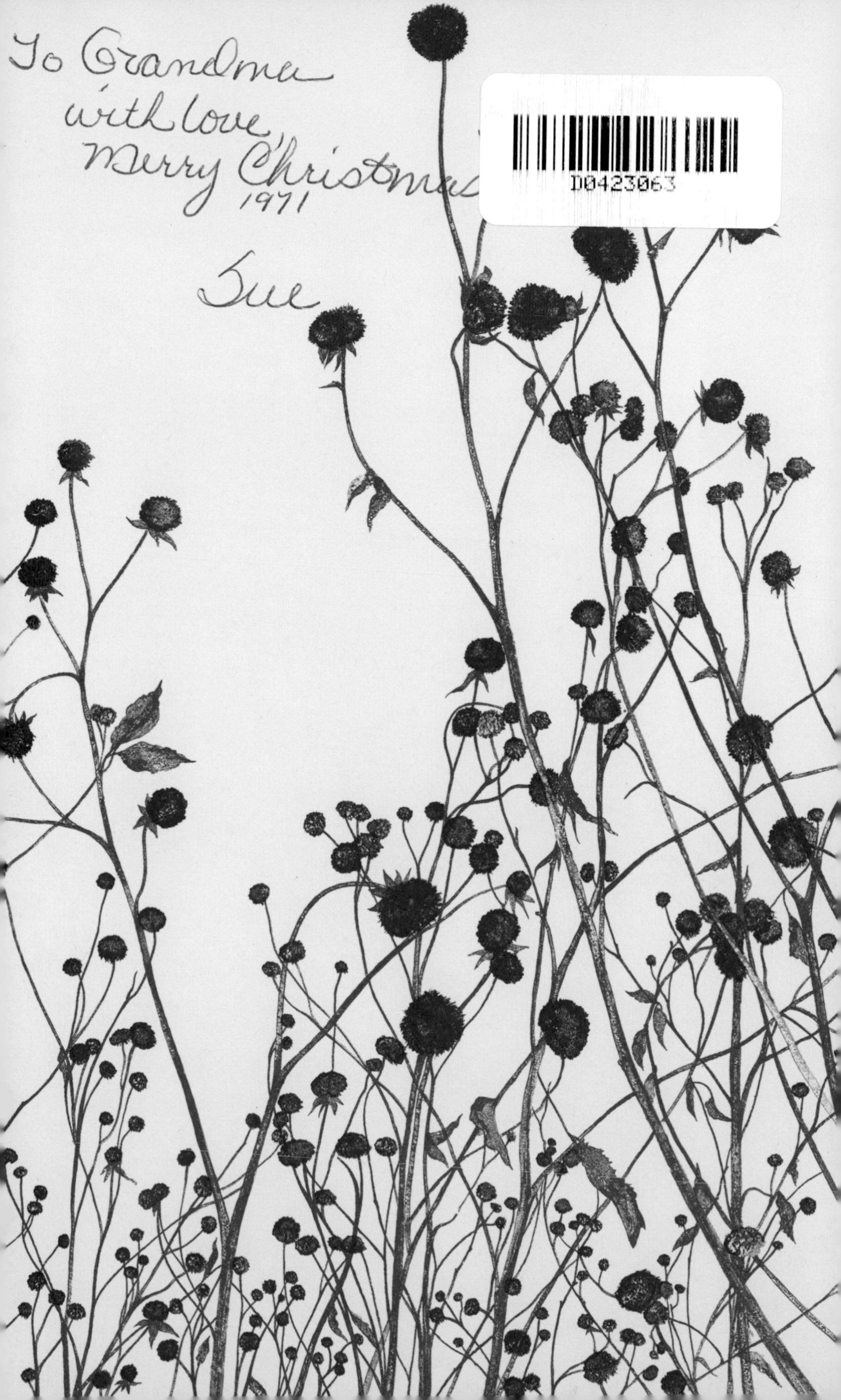

Pathways to Faith

By Dean Walley

Illustrated by Don Duhowski

Hallmark Crown Editions

Nature holds many pathways.......
.....bordered by flowers and ferns
that glisten with the morning dew.......
....covered with a mosaic
of brown and golden leaves........
......shaded by stately trees
that brush their branches
against the sky........
They are pathways to faith.

For the eternal truths
are not hidden in dark, forbidden places......
.....they appear with every step we take
on the pathways to faith.

Our faith is lifted up
and made strong
as we wander through a forest
where pine trees point to heaven.
They are silent children of earth.........
.......living towers of faith....
seeking a kinship with the sky.....

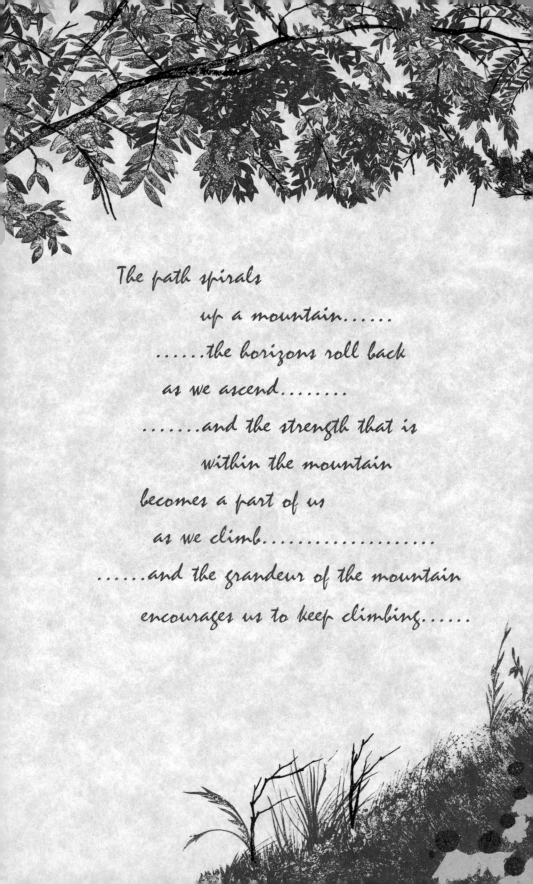

The path spirals
     up a mountain......
    ......the horizons roll back
as we ascend........
   ......and the strength that is
    within the mountain
becomes a part of us
  as we climb....................
......and the grandeur of the mountain
  encourages us to keep climbing......

In the purpose of nature
we begin to understand
the purpose of our own lives.....
.....and our faith is renewed.

On a summer day
we follow a pathway to a lazy meadow
sprinkled with buttercups........
........bees dart
from flower
to flower.....
....intent on the business
of gathering honey.....
....and we find faith
that the force that guides the bee
will direct our course as well.

The wind seems to blow capriciously.....

  ......but the wind reveals its purpose

   as invisible fingers pick up tiny seeds

  and scatter them

     over

      the

      earth.......

.....the wind's cool breath refreshes us

after the heat of the day.

   Sometimes it is heavy with fragrance....

  ......sometimes, moist with rain......

.....and as the wind's voice
sings through the forest.........
        ....calling out to all living things....
we respond to that call
and become one
        with the purpose of the wind.

Ahead of us
   ---suddenly----
a doe and her fawn streak across the path
and disappear in the forest....

....and the sight of these
beautiful creatures
who were born free
reminds us that we are also free.....
....free....
to embrace the faith that fills our existence
with purpose.

Sometimes our lives seem hurried
and chaotic........
    ....like geese beating the air
            with their wings......
.....invading the sky.
But geese soon arrow across the sky
    in grace and beauty......
        ....and seeing their passage
gives us faith in the order of life.......

We see the spider weaving its web
in silken symmetry.......
.....and we understand
how the pattern of our days
can be woven
from golden moments
into timeless beauty.

As the sun nourishes the earth,
the light of faith can nourish
our lives.........
.......and help us grow closer
to the Source of life.

As the moon pulls the tides......
the power of faith can cause our lives
to flow.............
.......out of oceans
of
turbulence and fear.........
toward quiet harbors of serenity.

Along nature's pathway
a fullness of love inspires our faith—
A divine love brushes the flowers
with indigo and vermillion............
.......contours the verdant hills.....
......burnishes the plains
with golden grain.

An eternal love gives us
the daily drama of sunset....
....spreading crimson over the horizon.......

.....and to dispel
the melancholy shadows of evening,
we have love's reminder—
—in a star.

A bird soars joyfully
across the sky..............

.......its beauty tells of a love
that is greater than all others.......
.....and our hearts find wings
with which to soar
to new heights of faith.

Across our path
a tree has fallen......
.....yet even in death
it has the promise of life.
For its life is flowing into the earth
from which it came......
and it is becoming tall grass
and violets......
it is changing
into velvety moss
and snow white mushrooms—
And so its life will go on.........

We see the promise
    of light and happiness
  in the miracle of sunrise.....
......and every beam warms our heart
like a smile of reassurance.

In the endless procession
of the seasons.........
...we see the assurance of the endless
cycle of life.....
...carrying us beyond the mystery....
.....into a place where the seasons
of the heart
will turn forever.

The pathways of nature take us to places
that no mortal can reveal to us.........
.......for they wind
through the beauty of the world.......
.......through the secrets of our own
hearts.......
drawing ever closer
to the Source of life.

And as the journey progresses,
our faith grows ever stronger--------
We find that we never see shadows.....
.....as long as we face the sun.........

.............and we understand
that the joy of our days
is truly unlimited.....
......when we look up, into the unknown.......

......and count the stars.

This book was designed and illustrated by Don Dubowski. The artist made his own color separations and closely supervised the printing for utmost accuracy of reproduction. The type is set in Minstral, an informal, true script designed in 1955 by Roger Excoffon for the Amsterdam Typefoundry. The paper is Hallclear, White Imitation Parchment and Ivory Fiesta Parchment. The cover is bound with imported natural Seta silk book cloth and Torino paper.